The **Ashok** Book of *Favourite*
Indian Recipes

 UBSPD

UBS Publishers' Distributors Ltd.
New Delhi Bombay Bangalore Madras
Calcutta Patna Kanpur London

UBS Publishers' Distributors Ltd.
5 Ansari Road, New Delhi-110 002
Bombay Bangalore Madras
Calcutta Patna Kanpur London

© India Tourism Development Corporation

First Published 1993

ISBN 81-85944-16-4

Editor   :   Chandni Luthra
Consulting Editor : Sudhir Kumar Sibal
Photographer   :   Sandeep Mathur
Coordinator   :   Vineeta Gogia

Cover design : UBS Art Studio

Lasertypeset in 11 pt. Garamond at Alphabets, N-22, South Extension, Part I, New Delhi
Printed at NUTECH PHOTOLITHOGRAPHERS SHAHDARA DELHI-110 095

Curry! But there is more to Indian food than curries. What we have in fact is a rich array of regional foods as diverse as the total European cuisine, with as many subtle flavours as the Chinese specialities. We have a culinary tradition that is passed down from generation to generation, enriched by master cooks who are often simply housewives, and rarely featuring in popular cook books.

In India there are dishes that are eaten only in summer or winter or during the monsoons. Through the ages daily food has been categorised as *Tamsik* (food that arouses passions and tempers), *Satvik* (nourishment that brings forth saintly qualities in man) or *Rajsik* (meals that feed noble and ambitious instincts). They are key words to ancient wisdom rooted in practice, and more often than not in science and commonsense, for eating the right kinds of food and staying healthy.

India is a land of spices which in the bygone ages lured traders and pioneers to its tropical shores. Understanding the generic word curry, opens the door to a rich storehouse of spices, the basic ones being coriander, turmeric, cumin seed, fenugreek, black pepper and red chilly powder. Often these basic spices are mixed with some others like mustard, anise, poppy and caraway seeds and so on, adding a dash of nutmeg, mace, cardamom, cloves and cinnamon to add that elusive taste to food. There is a liberal use of onion, garlic and ginger in most Indian cooking, not all.

It is said that the art of Indian cooking is always in the hands which cleverly blend various ingredients and spices bringing out flavours and aromas that tickle the palate. There are the masterly additions like almonds or cashewnuts ground to paste, onions browned to crisp, the whiff of saffron and other special touches that are so typical of northern India. In the south, there is a marked preference for the lighter touch of curry leaves, yoghurt, tamarind and coconut flavours. From northern Himalayas to the southern tip of India, from the north-eastern States to the west, there are such a profusion of mouthwatering savouries and sweets to be relished that it would be difficult to say precisely what is the national cuisine of India. The variety of cereals and lentils are unlimited. It is said that there are at least 200 types of rice and the daily bread comes in different forms -- stuffed, fried, flaked, baked in a mud oven, toasted over an open fire and even tossed in the air to make it handkerchief thin.

A typical *thali* is therefore a platter containing small bowl of lentil, vegetables, yoghurt, salad, pickles and a dessert which together constitute a well-balanced nutrition that ensures good health despite extremes of climate. Non-vegetarian dishes are as numerous as the vegetarian, with the famous tandoori chicken and meat prominently starring on menus of Indian restaurants popular around the world. Their old Mughal recipes are today closely guarded secrets of famous restaurants and old families.

The Ashok Group has a chain of hotels and restaurants, offering between them every major regional speciality. With more than 25 years of expertise, the Ashok Group of Hotels have promoted Indian cuisine in the world market by participating in food festivals of many countries. Our master chefs have also served royalty and heads of government at prestigious international gatherings.

In this book, the chefs of the Ashok Group offer you some of our choicest recipes to make eating an experience, and to add new spice to your life.

New Delhi

(Anil Bhandari)
Chairman & Managing Director
India Tourism Development Corporation

Introduction

India is well known the world over for its variety of cuisines which are slowly becoming more and more popular in other countries. The Ashok Group's restaurants in its 35 hotels endeavour to serve the choicest international and regional menus.

To serve a perfect meal, it is important to pay attention to details like visual appeal, texture, aroma, taste and nutrition value. When we plan a complete meal we first look for dishes which will have eye appeal. An array of dishes in various natural colours builds up an appetite and a variety of textures from gravies to dry recipes creates an interest, specially if the garnishing is imaginatively decorative. The preparation and the aroma of each dish either sustains the interest or diminishes it. When you taste the meal the taste can last forever in your mind, leaving behind a memory of something unique and exotic.

The nutritious value of each dish and the mixing of proteins, carbohydrates, fats, etc., is also something that dieticians or chefs cannot ignore. If a meal leaves you hungry for more it is actually well planned and cooked and easy to digest.

From appetizers like *Jaljira, Amras* to entrees, main dishes, rotis, rice, desserts and coffee, and then the digestive served in the form of saunf, supari and paans, it is important to plan your meal step by step.

In the Ashok Hotels every menu is carefully planned in every restaurant to ensure that the customer has a meal that is unforgettable and leaves behind a taste that craves for more.

In this recipe book we have select recipes from different regions. To make an exciting and complete meal include an appetizer, a salad, a yoghurt, vegetables, meats, breads, rice and a dessert. Papad, chutneys and pickles add to its grandeaur. Pick dishes from the north, south, east and west and mix'n match for the best results.

Our chefs have added a special touch to each recipe which will make it different from the rest and give it an exclusive 'Ashok' flavour.

Bon Appetit,

Chittra

CHANDNI LUTHRA
Vice-President
India Tourism Development Corporation

How to use this book

The recipes in this book have been collected from all over the regions, a true representation of various cuisines and have been classified into five major categories:

Starters, non-vegetarian, vegetarian, Indian breads and mithai (dessert).

To simplify cooking, the ingredients in this book have been listed in order in which they are to be used except for the main ingredient. If available, the ingredients, as a rule, should be fresh and seasonal, as the fresh ingredients do assist in bringing out the right texture, colour, aroma and taste of the delicacy.

The ingredients in this recipes should be used in the exact proportion and quantity in the sequence specified. All weights and measures used are 'Net' and not 'Gross'. The quantities are given in metric system. For convenient conversions, 1 tsp (tea spoon) may be taken as 5 gm, and 1 tbs (table spoon) as 3 tsp or 15 gm.

Each recipe yields four full portions except for Indian breads. When preparing a menu, avoid taking two dishes from the same style of cooking.

An ideal Indian menu should have a starter or a kabab to start with, followed by a fish or a chicken dish, a lamb dish, a vegetable and a lentil alongwith the usual accompaniments and finished with a dessert. Be sure to draw a balance between the gravy and the dry dishes, as also the colour of the dishes.

Indian cooking demands a range of pots and pans of various shapes and sizes usually of copper, brass and earthenware but now-a-days stainless steel or alloys are used. North Indian traditional clay oven, 'TANDOOR', is probably the most versatile kitchen equipment in the world and is fired by charcoal. The other commonly used utensils in Indian cooking are three—*handi, kadhai* and *tawa*. Though sizes and shapes merely differ, but a common feature is thick bottom to ensure that the food does not stick and consequently burn.

SUDHIR KUMAR SIBAL
Executive Chef

Contents

VEGETARIAN

BREADS

DESSERTS

Aam Pana

A Tangy Delicious Drink made from Raw Mangoes

Ingredients	
Raw Mangoes	1 kg
Sugar	250 gm
Rock Salt	5 gm
Cumin Seeds	15 gm
Salt	To taste
Lemon	2 nos.
Mint Leaves	5 sprigs
Water	600 ml

Preparation time : 30 minutes

Cooking time : 1 hour

Yield : 4

Preparation

Clean and wash the mangoes in running water. Broil cumin seeds and powder them. Pound rock salt. Clean and wash mint leaves. Cut lemon into half, remove seeds and extract juice.

Cooking

Roast raw mangoes on charcoal fire or even with foil till cooked. Peel them off and then pass gently through running water without disturbing the pulp. In an earthenware pitcher/glass jar, take pulp of the cooked mangoes after removing the seed. Mix with cold water, add sugar, rock salt and roasted cumin seed powder. Mix properly. Add lemon juice and salt.

To Serve

Serve chilled in khullar (earthenware tumbler)/ high ball glass and decorate with mint leaves.

Ashok Hotel, New Delhi

Moru Vellam

A Salted Refreshing South Indian Yoghurt Drink

Ingredients

Yoghurt	400 gm
Salt	To taste
Green Chillies	1 tsp
Ginger	A little
Curry Leaves	1 sprig
Citrus Leaves	A few
Mustard Seeds	1 tsp
Water	800 ml
Oil	1 tsp

Preparation time : 10 minutes

Yield : 4

Preparation

Beat yoghurt with salt and mix with water to make four glasses of Moru Vellam.

To Serve

Heat oil in a pan. Add mustard seeds. When the seeds crackle, add finely chopped green chillies, ginger, curry leaves, citrus leaves. Add to Moru Vellam. Serve chilled.

Kovalam Ashok Beach Resort, Kovalam.

The Ashok Book of Favourite Indian Recipes

Beler Serbat (Wood Apple Drink)

A Sweet, Cooling Wood Apple Drink

Ingredients	
Ripe Wood Apple	4 nos
Milk or Water	1 litre
Sugar	To taste

Preparation time : 20 minutes

Yield : 4

Preparation

Break the ripe wood apple and remove the seeds and surrounding gum-like substance.

Mash the fleshy portion. In a blender put the fleshy portion, sugar, chilled milk or water and mix well.

To Serve

Strain the liquid into a glass. Serve chilled.

Hotel Airport Ashok, Calcutta.

Karbuja Panakam

Watermelon Sherbat

Ingredients	
Watermelon	1 small no.
Sugar	100 gm
Ginger	5 gm
Salt	1/4 tsp
Cardamon Powder	1/2 tsp

Preparation time : 15 minutes

Yield : 4

Preparation

Scrape, skin out water melon and mash the pulp to make a paste, strain through muslin to extract juice. Add mashed water melon, ginger juice, cardamom powder, salt to the juice.

To Serve

Serve Chilled

Hotel Ashok, Bangalore.

Achari Winglets

Tempting Pickled Chicken Winglets

Ingredients	
Chicken Winglets	12 nos.
Chicken Mince	150 gm
Garam Masala	2 gm
Coriander Leaves	5 gm
Ginger Paste	5 gm
Garlic Paste	5 gm
Red Chilli Powder	3 gm
Salt	To taste
Mixed Pickle Mixture	40 gm
Refined Oil	To fry
For Batter	
Cornflour	40 gm
Saffron	1 gm
Water	100 ml

Preparation time : 45 minutes

Cooking time : 20 minutes

Yield : 4

Preparation

Scrape the flesh from the bone of the winglets, taking care to leave a little towards the end.

Mix chicken mince, garam masala, chopped coriander leaves, ginger-garlic paste, red chilli powder and salt.

Make a batter of cornflour, saffron and water. Keep aside.

Cooking

Stuff the mixture into chicken winglet flesh. Dip in batter and fry in hot oil till golden brown.

To serve

Coat with mixed pickle mixture and serve hot on a bed of onion rings.

Ashok Hotel, New Delhi.

Mint Chutney

A Tangy and Spicy Mint Chutney

Ingredients	
Mint Leaves (Fresh)	200 gm
Coriander Leaves	100 gm
Green Chillies	10 gm
Salt	To taste
Pomegranate Seeds (Dry)	10 gm
Yoghurt	50 gm
Tepid Water	20 ml

Preparation time: 15 minuts

Yield : 4

Preparation

Remove the mint and coriander leaves from the stems and wash well. Clean and chop green chillies, soak pomegranate seeds in tepid water for 10 minutes. Remove from water before using. Beat the yoghurt.

Method

Grind the mint and coriander leaves, green chillies, pomegranate seeds and salt. Add whipped yoghurt and mix well.

To Serve

Serve chilled

Ashok Hotel, New Delhi.

Chicken Chaat

A Delectable Spicy Chicken Savoury

Ingredients

Chicken (800 gms)	1 no.
Garlic Paste	30 gm
Dry Mango Powder	5 gm
Salt	To taste
Pepper	3 gm
Oil	20 ml
Capsicum	50 gm
Onion	50 gm
Tomatoes	50 gm
Lemon Juice	2 nos.
Red Chilli Powder	3 gm
Black Salt	2 gm
Chopped Coriander	5 gm
Chopped Green Chillies	4-5 nos
Chaat Masala	6 gm

Preparation time : 2 hours

Cooking time : 10 minutes

Yield : 4

Preparation

Clean and de-skin the chicken, make slits on the surface with a sharp knife. Make a paste of oil, mango powder, salt, pepper and garlic. Apply this paste evenly over the chicken. Marinate for 2 hours.

Deseed capsicum and tomatoes. Cut these and onion into roughly 1" cubes. Keep capsicum and onion in chilled water to ensure crispness.

Cooking

Roast the chicken in a hot oven for 25-30 minutes. Remove and cool. Separate the flesh from the bone and cut into 1" cubes. Sprinkle with black salt and juice of one lemon. Allow to cool.

To Serve

Put the chicken, capsicum, onion and tomatoes in a mixing bowl. Add the juice of one lemon, chilli powder, coriander, green chillies and the chaat masala and toss well using 10 ml of extra oil for the glaze. Adjust seasoning. Serve on a salad plate decorated with slices of tomatoes, cucumber and lemon.

Ashok Hotel, New Delhi.

Chillah

Gram-flour Pancakes

Ingredients
The Batter

Gramflour	300 gm
Salt	to taste
Cumin Seeds	4 gm
Red Chilli Powder	3 gm
Asafoetida	1.5gm/a very generous pinch
Refined Oil	To shallow fry

The Topping

Cottage Cheese	150 gm
Onions	80 gm
Tomatoes	75 gm
Coriander	12.5 gm
Green Chillies	2

Preparation Time: 25 minutes

Cooking Time: 2 minutes per Chillah

Yield : 4

Preparation : *Gramflour* : Sift alongwith salt into a bowl, add seeds and red chillies, mix well.

The Asafoetida: Dissolve in 45 ml of water.

The Batter: Mix the dissolved asafoetida and 540 ml of water with the besan mixture and make a batter of pouring consistency. Divide into 16 equal portions and keep aside.

The Cottage Cheese: Grate, mash or make small dices and divide into 16 portions.

The Vegetable: Peel onions, wash and make small dices. Remove eyes, wash tomatoes, quarter, deseed and make small dices. Clean, and finely chop coriander. Remove stems, wash, slit, deseed and finely chop green chillies. Mix all the ingredients in a bowl and divide into 16 equal portions.

Cooking : Heat just enough clarified butter or refined oil in a small frying pan, spread a portion of the batter to make a pancake with a 4" diameter and shallow fry over low heat for a few seconds. Then sprinkle a portion each of the cottage cheese and vegetables over the surface of the pancake, sprinkle a little oil along the peripherry and cook. Lift the pancake and, if perforations are visible and the Chillah is lightly coloured, flip it over. Sprinkle another small quantity of oil and cook for 45 seconds. Fold and remove to absorbent paper to drain off the excess fat. Repeat the process with the remaining portions.

To Serve : Remove to a dish and serve with coriander (60%) — Mint (40%) — Chutney or *saunth* and accompaniments of your choice.

Ashok Hotel, New Delhi.

Dahi Kabab

A Unique Subtly Flavoured Yoghurt Kabab

Ingredients

Well-set Yoghurt	250 gm
Cottage Cheese	50 gm
White Pepper	2 gm
Coriander Leaves	10 gm
Green Chillies	2 gm
Garam Masala	1 tsp
Salt	To taste
Refined Oil	To fry
Corn Flour	30 gm

Preparation time : 3 hours

Cooking time : 20 minutes

Yield : 4

Preparation

Hang yoghurt in a muslin cloth in a cool place until completely drained of whey, (approx. 3 hrs). Mix well the yoghurt and cottage cheese. Wash and finely chop coriander leaves and green chillies. Slit and deseed green chillies before chopping them. Add to yoghurt and cottage cheese mixture. Add garam masala and salt. Kneed to make a soft dough with corn flour. Make small *Tikkis* and keep aside.

Cooking

Heat oil in a heavy bottomed pan and shallow fry the *Tikkis* over medium heat until golden brown and crisp on both sides. Press with a spatula and remove.

To Serve

Arrange the *Tikkis* on a platter and serve with mint chutney.

Ashok Hotel, New Delhi

Crab Masala

A piece de resistance among non-vegetarian recipes

Ingredients

Crabs	1 kg
Onion	200 gm
Ginger	15 gm
Garlic	5 gm
Tomato	120 gm
Coconut	½ no.
Tamarind	10 gm
Cumin Seeds	5 gm
Turmeric Powder	2 gm
Red Chilli Powder	2 gm
Coriander Powder	2 gm
Garam Masala	3 gm
Oil	30 ml
Water	60 ml

Preparation time : 1 hour 30 minutes

Cooking time : 25 minutes

Yield : 4

Preparation

Put the crabs in a bowl of hot water to calm them. Now pull off the claws, legs and lift up the flap on the underside to open the crabs. Clean and discard the portion around the eyes. Also discard the spongy matter on the fleshier side. Boil the crabs. Finely chop onions, make ginger-garlic paste. Chop tomatoes. Extract tamarind juice. Grate and grind coconut with cumin seeds.

Cooking

Heat oil and fry onion till golden brown. Add ginger-garlic paste and tomatoes. Add turmeric powder, red chilli powder and coriander powder. Add ground coconut paste, water and salt. Add tamarind juice and cook on slow fire. Add crab meat, cook till done, sprinkle garam masala, stir and remove. Adjust seasoning.

To Serve

Serve crab masala with rice.

Kovalam Ashok Beach Resort, Kovalam.

Chippi Theeyal

A Coconut flavoured mussel curry simmered in a delicately spiced gravy

Ingredients

Mussels	48 no.
Small Red Onions	50 gm
Turmeric Powder	2 gm
Salt	To taste
Coconut	½ no.
Red Chilli Powder	3 gm
Coriander Powder	2 gm
Cumin Seeds	5 gm
Garlic	15 gm
Oil	30 ml
Coconut Oil	15 ml
Red Chilli Whole	6 nos.
Mustard Seeds	2 gm
Curry Leaves	A sprig

Preparation Time : 2 hours

Cooking Time : 30 minutes

Yield: 4

Preparation

Wash split mussels and take out the flesh. Clean and remove sand fully. Cut into small pieces. Chop small red onions. Grate coconut. Chop garlic. Heat half the oil and fry coconut, add red chilli powder, coriander powder, turmeric powder, cumin seeds and garlic to golden brown and grind.

Cooking

Heat the remaining oil and fry chopped red onions. Add turmeric powder, salt, mussels and water. Simmer. Add ground masala and cook. Remove from fire.

To Serve

Heat the coconut oil and add mustard seeds, red chilli whole and curry leaves. When it is brown, add to the cooked mussel curry and adjust seasoning. Serve hot with rice.

Kovalam Ashok Beach Resort, Kovalam

Jhinga Malai Cream

Subtly Spiced Prawns Laced with Cream

Ingredients	
Prawns	1 kg
Coconut	2 nos.
Cream	50 ml
Curd	100 ml
Onion	200 gm
Ginger	15 gm
Garlic	15 gm
Garam Masala	1 tsp
Salt	To taste
Red Chilli Powder	3 gm
Oil	50 ml
Curry Leaves	2 nos
Cumin Seeds	1 tsp
Water	100 ml

Preparation time : 30 minutes

Cooking time : 20 minutes

Yield : 4

Preparation

Shell prawns. Devein and wash in water. Extract coconut milk. Cut and slice onion. Make ginger-garlic paste.

Cooking

Heat oil, add cumin seeds, fry till they crackle. Now add sliced onions, curry leaves, ginger-garlic paste and fry till golden brown in colour.

Add curd, red chilli powder, salt and garam masala. Then, add prawns and water. Cook for 5 minutes. Adjust seasoning.

To serve

Turn onto a serving dish lace with a mixture of coconut milk and cream. Sprinkle garam masala on top and serve hot.

Ashok Hotel, New Delhi.

Tandoori Machhi

Spiced Tandoori Pomfret

Ingredients	
Pomfret	4 nos.
(each weighing 300 gms)	
Carom Seeds (Ajwain)	15 gm
Gram Floor	10 gm
Yoghurt	60 gm
Egg	1 no.
Red Chilli Powder	5 gm
Dried Fenugreek Leaves	5 gm
Salt	To taste
Vinegar	15 ml
Ginger	20 gm
Garlic	20 gm
Chaat Masala	10 gm
Onion	50 gm
Tomatoes	30 gm
Cucumber	30 gm
Lemon	1 no.
Mint Chutney	80 ml

Preparation time : 2 hours

Cooking time : 20 minutes

Yield : 4

Preparation

Remove fins, eyes and clean the stomach. Clean with vinegar water. Make ginger-garlic paste. Marinate yoghurt mixed with gram flour, egg, red chilli powder, carom seeds, dried fenugreek leaves, salt, ginger-garlic paste.

Cooking

Arrange on skewer. Cook in a hot tandoor till done.

To serve

Remove from skewer. Sprinkle chaat masala on top. Garnish with onion rings, tomato slices, cucumber slices, lemon wedges. Accompanied with mint chutney.

Ashok Hotel, New Delhi.

Ilish Mach Bhapa (Steamed Hilsha)*

Mustard-Flavoured Steamed Fish

Ingredients:

Ilish/Mackeral	8 pieces
(75 gms each piece)	
Mustard Oil	5 tbs
Grated Coconut	2 tbs
Green Chilli	5 nos.
Mustard Seeds	3 tsp
Turmeric Powder	1 tsp
Salt	To taste

Preparation Time : 45 minutes

Cooking Time : 20 minutes

Yield : 4

Preparation

Wash, clean and descale the Hilsha fish and cut into darne of 3/4" thickness. Wash and keep aside. Make a paste of 3 nos. green chilly, mustard seeds, grated coconut and salt.

Cooking

In a container having a lid, put the fish pieces and the spice paste, mustard oil, salt, turmeric powder and 2 nos. slit, green chillies. Mix well, put the lid on the container. In another bigger pan, heat some water and put the closed container having the fish. Make sure the water level is below the lid level so that water cannot get inside the fish container. Keep on a simmering flame for about 10 minutes. Open the container. Adjust seasoning.

To serve

Remove into a serving dish. Serve hot with steamed rice.

Hotel Airport Ashok, Calcutta.

---

* Mackeral is having almost the same kind of flavour as Hilsha and as a substitute 'Mackeral' fish can be used.

Kozhi Saaru

A Traditional & Delectable Chicken Curry — Karnataka Style

Ingredients	
Chicken	1 kg
The Gravy	
Cooking Oil	60 ml
Onion	100 gm
Ginger	10 gm
Garlic	15 gm
Coriander Powder	2 tbs
Red Chilli Powder	1 tsp
Turmeric Powder	1/2 tsp
Tomato	100 gm
Cinnamon	3 nos.
Cloves	5 nos.
Cardamom	5 nos.
Coconut Paste	1 tbs
Poppy Seeds	5 gm
Mint	1 small bunch
Coriander Leaves	1 small bunch
Water	250 ml
Salt	to taste

Preparation time : 1 hour

Cooking time : 30 minutes

Yield : 4

Preparation

Chicken : Clean, trim and cut chicken into small pieces and keep it aside. Peel, and slice onions. Make paste of poppyseeds, coconut, ginger and garlic.

Method

Heat oil in a heavy bottomed pan. Add cinnamon, cloves and cardamom and fry for a minute. Add sliced onion and fry till light golden brown. Add chicken to this browned onion masala. Cook it for 15 to 20 minutes. Add coriander powder, red chilli powder, poppy seed paste, coconut paste, ginger and garlic paste, turmeric powder, salt. Add water to the chicken masala. After cooking for 10 minutes, add tomato, chopped mint and coriander leaves. Simmer it for 2 minutes. Adjust the seasoning.

To serve

Hot with rice or roti.

Hotel Ashok Bangalore

Neza Kabab

A Unique Spicy Chicken Kabab Dressed in Creamy Yoghurt

Ingredients

Chicken leg	8 nos.
Yoghurt	200 gm
Gram Flour	100 gm
Cream	50 gm
Garlic Paste	10 gm
Ginger Paste	10 gm
Red Chilli Powder	1 tsp
Garam Masala Powder	1 tsp
Green Chillies	2 nos.
Green Coriander	20 gm
Green Cardamom Powder	2 gm
Salt	To taste
Oil	50 gm
Grated Cheese	10 gm

Preparation time : 1 hour 30 minutes

Cooking time : 20 minutes

Yield : 4

Preparation

Scrape flesh from the hind end of the leg tili 1/2" of the other end. Remove tendon and flatten it with the back of the knife. Hang yoghurt in muslin cloth for 30 minutes. Broil gram flour for one minute. Make ginger-garlic paste. Wash and chop coriander leaves and green chillies. Now slit and deseed the chopped green chillies. Grate cheese. Marinate the chicken in 150 gm yoghurt mixed with ginger-garlic paste, gram flour, red chillies powder and garam masala.

Cooking

Roast in tandoor. When it is 3/4th done, apply the remaining yoghurt, cream and cheese on the chicken lightly.

To Serve

Serve with mint chutney, onion rings and lemon wedges.

Ashok Hotel, New Delhi.

Natti Kabab

A tender kabab made from chicken mince, combined with herbs and cashewnuts. A Chef's original.

Ingredients	
Chicken Mince	800 gm
Ginger Paste	15 gm
Garlic Paste	15 gm
Garam Masala Powder	3 gm
Cashewnuts	50 gm
Red Cherry	10 pcs
Butter	50 gm
White Pepper	5 gm
Egg yolk	8 nos.
Salt	To taste
Onion	100 gm
Cucumber	100 gm
Tomatoes	100 gm
Lemons	4 nos.
Mint Leaves	100 gm
Coriander Leaves	40 gm
Green Chillies	10 gm
Yoghurt	100 ml

Preparation time : 30 minutes

Cooking time : 10 minutes

Yield : 4

Preparation

Make chicken mince and ginger-garlic paste. Mix it with garam masala and white pepper. Grate cashewnuts, finely chop red cherry. Mix with egg yolk. Make balls and keep aside. Slice onion, cucumber, tomato. Make mint chutney.

Cooking

Using a wet hand, spread the balls by pressing each along the length of the skewers 2" apart and making each kabab 5" long. Roast in a moderately hot tandoor for 10 minutes, brushing once with oil (basting) until they are golden brown. In a charcoal grill, cook for about the same time, basting once and in a pre-heated oven, roast for 10 minutes, basting once.

To Serve

Serve hot with onion rings, tomato and cucumber slices, lemon wedges, accompanied with mint chutney.

Ashok Hotel, New Delhi.

Uttar-Dakshin Murghbandi

A Unique North-South 'Jugal-Bandi' of Chicken Delicacy

Ingredients

Breast of Chicken	8
Flour	To dust
Cooking oil	To shallow fry

The Marination

Lemon Juice	30 ml
Garlic Paste	10gm
Ginger Paste	10gm
Coriander Powder	1.5gm
Red Chilli Powder	1.5gm
Turmeric Powder	1.5gm
Salt	To taste

The Filling

Chicken Mince	250gm
Cooking Oil	45gm
Asafoetida	A Pinch
Mustard Seeds	1.5gm
Curry Leaves	16
Madras Onions	30gm
Coconut	30gm
Cheese (processed/cheddar)	60gm
Salt	To taste

Preparation Time : 1.45 hours

Cooking Time : 1 hour

Yield : 4

Preparation

The Chicken: Clean, remove the skin, debone but retain the winglet bone, trim, wash and pat dry. With a sharp knife, pressing the supreme at the thicker end gently, slit the deboned breasts horizontally to make pockets ensuring that a third of the opposite side is left uncut.

The Martination: Mix all the ingredients, evenly smear the supremes with this marinade and reserve for 30 minutes.

The Filling: Clean and wash curry leaves. Peel, wash and chop onions. Remove the brown skin and grate coconut. Grate cheese.

Heat oil in a frying pan, add asafoetida, stir over medium heat until it swells up, add mustard seeds and curry leaves, stir until the seeds begin to crackle. Then add the onions and fry until translucent and glossy. Now add the chicken mince and salt, stir-fry until the moisture evaporates. Remove, cool, add coconut and cheese, mix well. Divide into 8 equal portions.

The Gravy: Peel, wash and chop onions. Soak saffron in lukewarm milk.

The Stuffing: Pack a portion of the filling in the pockets of the marinated chicken breasts and then seal each with the tip of the knife ensuring that the meat is not pierced. Dust the supremes with flour and keep aside.

The Gravy	
Clarified Butter	45 gm
Green Cardamom	5 nos.
Cloves	3 nos.
Black Cardamom	2 nos.
Cinnamon (1-inch)	2 sticks
Bay Leaf	1 no.
Madras Onions	60 gm
Garlic Paste	10 gm
Ginger Paste	10 gm
Coriander Powder	1.5 gm
Red Chilli Powder	1.5 gm
Turmeric Powder	1.5 gm
Salt	to taste
Poppy Seed Paste	30gm
Coconut Milk	180ml
Saffron	1gm
Milk	30 ml
The Garnish	
Green Peppercorns	10g
Tomoto	1 no.
Coriander	4 sprigs

The Garnish: Remove stems, clean, wash and pat dry green peppercorns. (Using canned peppercorns, drain the brine and pat dry). Remove eyes, wash tomato, halve, deseed and cut into small dices. Clean and wash coriander.

Cooking

Heat oil in a frying pan, add the stuffed supremes, two at a time, and fry over low heat, turning a couple of times, until evenly golden (approx 4-5 minutes). Then cover and cook, turning at regular intervals, for 2-3 minutes.

To prepare the gravy, heat clarified butter in a heavy bottomed pan, add green cardamom cloves, black cardamom, cinnamon and bay leaf, stir over medium heat until the green cardamom begins to change colour, add onions, until over medium heat until onions are translucent and glossy, add the garlic and ginger pastes, stir-fry until the moisture evaporates. (ensure that the masala does not get coloured). Then add coriander, red chilli and turmeric powders, stir, add the poppy seed paste, stir-fry until the fat begins to leave the sides (ensure that the masala does not get coloured), add the supremes and 400 ml of water, bring to a boil, reduce to low heat, simmer until the liquor is reduced by half. Remove the chicken supremes and keep aside. Pass the liquor through a fine mesh soups strainer into a separate pan. Return gravy to heat, add coconut milk and simmer until of sauce consistency. Add saffron, stir, remove and adjust the seasoning.

To serve

Arrange 2 supremes on each of 4 individual plates, pour on equal quantities of sauce, garnish with green peppercorns, tomato dices and coriander.

Ashok Hotel, New Delhi.

The Ashok Book of Favourite Indian Recipes

Murg Biryani Masaledar

A Spicy Rice & Chicken Delicacy, easy to digest

Ingredients	
Basmati Rice	200 gm
Chicken	750 gm
Onions	100 gm
Ginger	10 gm
Garlic	10 gm
Green Chillies	4 nos
Cumin Seeds	3 gm
Cardamom Green	5 nos
Cardamom Black	5 gm
Cloves	5 nos
Nutmeg Powder	1 gm
Aniseed Powder	1 gm
Coriander Powder	5 gm
Turmeric Powder	3 gm
Red Chilli Powder	2 gm
Bay Leaf	2 nos.
Salt	To taste
Oil	100 ml
Chicken Stock	250 ml
Tomatoes	150 gm
Fried Onions	30 gm
Green Coriander	5 gm
Mint	5 gm
Milk	30 ml

Preparation time : 1 hour

Cooking time : 45 minutes

Yield : 4

Preparation : Pick and wash basmati rice and soak in cold water for 1/2 hr. Deskin, cut chicken into pieces with bone. Make ginger-garlic paste. Slit, deseed and chop green chillies. Chop coriander, tomatoes, mint and onions. Deskin, slice onion and deep fry them in oil. Drain it on an absorbent paper.

Method : Heat oil, add the bay leaf, cardamom, cinnamon and cloves. Now add the cumin seeds and as soon as they start crackling, add the choped onions, fry till golden brown. Now add the ginger, garlic, red chillies, coriander powder, turmeric, salt and tomatoes. Cook well for 20-25 minutes using a little chicken stock to prevent the masala from sticking at the bottom. When the masala leaves the oil, add the chicken pieces and toss well till the masala evenly coats the chicken. Add the remaining stock and cook the chicken till half done. Simultaneously boil rice in double the quantity of cold water with some salt and 10 ml of oil. Drain the water when the rice is half cooked. Separate the chicken pieces from the masala and arrange these at the bottom of a thick bottomed pot. Arrange half the steaming hot rice over this. Sprinkle the nutmeg and aniseeds powder on top. Spread the masala over this layer and then the remaining rice. Spread the top of this with the chopped coriander and mint and browned sliced onions. Sprinkle milk on top, put a lid. Seal the edges of the lid using a little flour dough. Put in a hot oven for 20-25 mts.

To Serve : Remove the lid and serve hot.

Ashok Hotel, New Delhi.

Khatta Gosht

A Piquant and a Unique Smoky Flavoured Mutton Preparation

Ingredients

Mutton (Leg/Shoulder)	1 kg
Onion	150 gm
Ginger	30 gm
Garlic	30 gm
Tomatoes	150 gm
Pomegranate Seeds	100 gm
Jaggery	50 gm
Cloves	6 nos.
Cardamom	6 nos.
Bay Leaves	4 nos.
Fenugreek Seeds	1 tsp
Asafoetida	2 gm
Red Chilli Powder	1 tsp
Coriander Powder	1 tsp
Salt	To taste
Fat (preferably Mustard Oil)	50 ml
Cinnamon (1" stick)	2 nos.
Turmeric Powder	1/4 tsp

Preparation time : 30 minutes

Cooking time : 60 minutes

Yield : 4

Preparation

Cut mutton into 1" pieces, discarding any excess fat. Slice the onions. Chop the ginger and garlic. Finely chop tomatoes or liquidize in blender. Soak pomegranate seeds in warm water. Discard water and grind to a fine paste. Dissolve Asafoetida in a little warm water.

Cooking

Heat fat in a thick-bottom pan. Add fenugreek seeds, cardamom, cloves, cinnamon and bay leaves. When fenugreek seeds start cracking, add the asafoetida taking care to cover the pan while doing this. Add onions and stir till they are brown evenly. Add ginger, garlic and mutton. Stir occasionally. When the mutton is 3/4th done, add tomatoes, turmeric, red chilly powder/coriander powder, and salt. After cooking for another 15 minutes, add pomegranate paste and jaggery. Simmer for 15 minutes. Adjust seasoning.

Tempering : Take a small piece of charcoal and hold it over a flame till red hot. Dip it in oil and return to flame. Plunge this flaming charcoal in the pan and cover with lid. This imparts a smoky flavour to the dish.

To Serve : Remove charcoal and garnish with finely chopped coriander.

Hotel Jammu Ashok, Jammu.

Raan Alishan

Truly a Chef's Original. A Dry Mutton Preparation with Rum

Ingredients

Lamb leg (weighing 1 kg)	2 nos.
Ginger Paste	5 gm
Garlic Paste	5 gm
Red Chilli Powder	5 gm
Vinegar	20 ml
Tomato	5 gm
Onion	100 gm
Cucumber	50 gm
Mint Chutney	120 ml
Lemon	2 nos.
Raw Papaya	5 gm
Rum	120 ml
Salt	To taste
Lamb Stock	2 litres
Garam Masala	5 gm
Oil	40 ml
Chaat Masala	2 tbs.

Preparation time : 3 hours

Cooking time : 2 hours

Yield : 4

Preparation

Clean lamb leg. Make raw papaya paste and ginger-garlic paste. Make the marination with oil, ginger-garlic paste, red chilly powder, vinegar, 60 mls rum and salt. Marinate the cleaned lamb leg for 3 hours.

Cooking

Grease the baking tray with high sides, arrange the marinated legs in it. Add enough stock to immerse one third of the legs and roast in the pre-heated oven for 90 minutes. Baste at regular intervals using the stock and turn occasionally for even colouring. When it is almost cooked, take it out and put on skewer and finish it on charcoal fire.

To Serve

Sprinkle Rum and chaat masala on top and serve it with onion rings, tomato slices, cucumber slices, lemon wedges.

Ashok Hotel, New Delhi

Mutton Kandhari

A Delectable Mutton Dish Flavoured with Saffron

Ingredients

Mutton Steak 1 kg (boneless mutton piece cut into 1 cubes)	
Yoghurt	150 gm
Ginger Paste	20 gm
Garlic Paste	20 gm
Red Chilli Powder	5 gm
Salt	To taste

The Gravy

Onion	500 gm
Cooking Oil	100 ml
Big Cardamom	5 nos
Cloves	5 nos
Green Cardamom	5 nos
Bay Leaf	2 nos.
Cinnamon	2 stick 1" each
Ginger	20 gm
Garlic	20 gm
Yellow Chilli Powder	5 gm
Curd	150 gm
Saffron	1 gm
Milk	30 ml
Black Peppercorns	20 nos.
Salt	to taste
Cashewnuts	50 gm
Cream	50 ml
Pomegranate Juice	200 ml (of 2 pomegranate medium size)

Preparation time : 3 hours 30 minutes

Cooking time : 1 hour

Yield : 4

Preparation : Clean, trim and cut the mutton in 1 inch shape. Mix all ingredients in a large bowl. Put the mutton steak with this marinade and keep aside for at least 3 hours.

The gravy : Peel, wash and slice onion. Whisk yoghurt in a bowl. Soak saffron in lukewarm milk and then crush the flakes with back of a spoon. Put peppercorns in a mortar and powder with the paste to obtain a coarse powder. Add cashewnut paste.

Cooking : Melt fat in a thick bottomed pan, add the mutton pieces and cook until evenly coloured. Remove and keep aside. Reserve the liquor and the fat. Heat oil in a thick bottomed pan and add cardamom, cloves, bay leaf, cinnamon. Stir until cardamom changes colour, add onions and fry until light golden colour and add cashewnut paste and fry until golden colour and then add the garlic and ginger paste and fry until moisture has evaporated, add yellow chillies, salt, stir for 30 minutes. Remove pan from heat, stir in yoghurt, return pan to heat and stir fry until the fat begins to leave the sides. Now add the reserved liquor and fat, add water, bring to boil, reduce to low heat. Add mutton pieces, simmer stirring occasionally after adding pomegranate juice. Sprinkle cardamom, saffron, black pepper. Stir. Adjust the seasoning.

To Serve: Serve hot laced with cream

Ashok Hotel, New Delhi.

Tagaru Masala

A mutton masala with a difference — done in a smooth sauce flavoured with fennel seeds — Karnataka style

Ingredients

Mutton Chops	600 gm
The Gravy	
Cooking Oil	60 ml
Onion	150 gm
Fennel Seeds	1 tsp
Ginger	10 gm
Garlic	15 gm
Coriander Powder	2 tbs
Green Chillies	10 nos.
Turmeric Powder	1/2 tsp
Mint	1 small bunch
Coriander Leaves	1 small bunch
Cinnamon	2 nos 1" stick
Cloves	2 nos.
Cardamom	2 nos.
Tomato	100 gm
Water	600 ml
Salt	to taste

Preparation time: 2 hours

Cooking time: 1 hours

Yield: 4

Preparation

Clean, trim, remove the side ribs of the mutton and then carefully scrape off the meat from the lower part of the bones. Peel, wash and chop the onion. Make paste of ginger, garlic and green chillies.

Method

Heat oil in a heavy bottomed pan. Add fennel seeds, cinnamon, cloves and cardamom and fry it for a minute. Add chopped onion and fry till light golden brown. Add mutton chops to the browned onion masala. Cook it for 15-20 minutes.

Add coriander powder, green chilli paste, turmeric powder, ginger and garlic paste, salt. Add water to the mutton chop masala. Add tomato after cooking for 30 minutes. Add chopped coriander and mint leaves. Adjust the seasoning. Simmer it for 15 minutes.

To Serve

Serve hot with rice or roti.

Hotel Ashok Bangalore.

Kali-Amba

An outstanding work of culinary art. Succulent pieces of mutton cooked in raw mangoes.

Ingredients	
Mutton	500 gm
Ghee	50 gm
Cloves	4 nos
Green Cardamom	6 nos
Cinnamon (1" piece)	2 pieces
Bay Leaf	2 nos.
Poppy Seeds	20 gm
Coconut Powder	20 gm
Turmeric Powder	3 gm
Red Chilli Powder	3 gm
Salt	To taste
Gravy	
Raw Mangoes	500 gm
Sugar	250 gm
Water	1 litre
Cashewnuts	20 gm
Almonds	20 gm
Makhanas (fried)	20 gm
Sunflower Seeds	20 gm
Dry Coconut	50 gm

Preparation Time : 2 hours

Cooking Time : 1 hour 30 minutes

Yield : 4

Preparation

Clean and cut mutton into cubes. Make poppy seed paste. Peel and cut mangoes into thick slices. Cook in a syrup of sugar and water till the mangoes are 3/4 th cooked and the syrup becomes thick. Keep aside. Coarsely chop cashewnuts, almonds and dry coconut.

Cooking

Heat oil in a pan. Add clove, cinnamon, cardamom and bay leaf. Cook till it gives aroma. Add mutton cubes and fry for 5 minutes. Add poppy seed paste and coconut powder. Cook the mixture for sometime, stirring all the time. Add turmeric powder, red chilli powder and salt. Cook for a few seconds and add water. Cook till the mutton becomes tender (almost cooked) and the gravy thickens. To this, add the mixture of mangoes, cooked in sugar syrup. Cook for 5 minutes and remove. Adjust seasoning.

To Serve

Transfer to a serving dish and garnish with cashewnuts, almonds, sunflower seeds, makhanas and dry coconut slices. Serve as a main dish accompanied with Sheermal.

Hotel Agra Ashok, Agra.

Handi Pasanda

A mutton delicacy napped in a masala rich in herbs and spices

Ingredients

Mutton Pasanda	24
(50 gms each; from the leg)	
The Marination	
Raw Papaya Paste	30 gm
Cashewnut Paste	
(from 20 nuts)	15 gm
Poppy Paste	15 gm
Sunflower Seed Paste	15 gm
Ginger Paste	20 gm
Garlic Paste	20 gm
The Gravy	
Cooking Oil	75 ml
Onion Paste	150 gm
Yoghurt	150 gm
Fried Onion Paste	150 gm
Garam Masala	3 gm
Salt	To taste
The Accompaniments	
Small Potatoes	24
Salt	to taste
Coriander Leaves	10 gm

Preparation times : 40 minutes

Cooking time : 1 hour

Yield : 4

Preparation : Obtain 55 gm cubes from the leg, clean and, using a bat, flatten them into 1/4- inch thick pieces of 4 inch diameter. Trim, wash and pat dry. Mix all the pastes tested under marination alone and rub the pasanda with it, making sure they are evenly coated. Keep aside for 30 minutes. Whisk yoghurt in a bowl. Boil, cool and peel potatoes. Clean, wash and finely chop all but 4 sprigs of coriander. Sprinkle salt on the potatoes, keep warm and roll them in the chopped coriander at the time of service. Fry sliced onion till golden brown, make a paste.

Cooking : Heat oil in a large heavy bottomed pan, add onion paste, stir-fry over medium heat until light golden. Add 3 gm red chillies; stir and remove pan from heat, stirring yoghurt, return to heat and bring to boil. Then arrange the pasanda in the pan — they may touch the sides but not cover or overlap — and stir carefully until the fat begins to appear on the surface. Now add fried onion paste, stir carefully, add salt, stir-reduce to low heat, cover with a lid and put on dum, stirring occasionally, but carefully, until cooked and the gravy is of a thin consistency. Remove, sprinkle garam masala, stir and adjust seasoning.

To Serve : Make a bed of equal quantities of sauce on each of 4 individual plates, arrange the pasanda, overlapping, in a flower shape. Place the potatoes around the "flower", arrange a sprig of coriander on the "flower" and serve with Tandoori Roti

Ashok Hotel, New Delhi.

The Ashok Book of Favourite Indian Recipes

Pandi Curry

A traditional Coorgi Pork Curry recipe cooked in a palate-tickling combination of vinegar, herbs and spices.

Ingredients

Pork	1 kg
Onion	300 gm
Ginger (Chopped)	15 gm
Green Chillies	15 nos
Coriander	100 gm
Cardamom	4 nos
Cloves	4 nos
Pepper Corn	10 nos
Cinnamon	2 nos 1" pieces
Cumin Seeds	1 tsp
Mustard Seeds	tsp
Oil	60 ml
Water	400 ml
Vinegar	1 tbs

Preparation time : 45 minutes

Cooking time : 1 hour

Yield : 4

Preparation

Debone the pork legs and remove the skin and excess fat. Cut into cubes. Make a paste of onions. Chop ginger and green chillies, grind coarsely. Separately broil coriander seeds till brown and finely powder. Broil and finely powder cardamom, cloves, pepper corn, cinnamon, cumin seeds and mustard seeds.

Cooking

Marinate pork with salt and turmeric for half an hour. Add the coarsely ground paste of onion, ginger and green chillies. Mix and keep for 15 minutes. Pour oil in a thick bottom pan; add marinated pork, and fry for 10 minutes. Pour enough water to cover the pork and cook it over slow fire till done. When cooked, add 1 tsp of garam masala and finish off with vinegar. Adjust seasoning.

To Serve

Serve hot with steamed rice.

Hotel Ashok, Bangalore.

Baida Kabab

An exotic Kabab made from eggs

Ingredients	
Egg	11 nos.
Onions	75 gm
Ginger	10 gm
Coriander	10 gm
Green Chillies	2 nos.
Stuffed Olives	8 nos.
Ginger Paste	10 gm
Garlic Paste	10 gm
Fresh Breadcrumbs	30 gm
Cornflour	10 gm
Chaat Masala	3 gm
White Pepper Powder	2 gm
Dried Fenugreek Leaves	1 gm
Blac Rock Salt	1 gm
Green Cardamom Powder	1 gm
Mace Powder	1 gm
Salt	To taste
Oil	100 ml
The Accompaniments	
Egg (boiled)	2 nos.
Aubergines(cumin tempered)	4 nos.

Preparation time : 45 minutes

Cooking time: 7-10 minutes

Yield : 4

Preparation : Three-quarter boil (approx 6 minutes) 9 eggs, cool, shell and grate (do not mash) into a bowl. Break the remaining eggs and mix with the boiled eggs. Peel, wash and finely chop onions. Scrape, wash and finely chop ginger. Clean, wash and chop coriander. Remove stems, wash, slit, deseed and finely chop green chillies. Finely chop the olives. Powder dried fenugreek leaves. Put rock salt in a mortar and pound with a pestle to obtain fine powder. Mix well with rock salt powder fenugreek leaves powder. Add all the ingredients to the eggs, except the accompaniments, and mix well. (Add more breadcrumbs, if necessary, to get the right consistency: dry-not sticky-like mashed potatoes. Divide into 16 equal portions and make balls. Pre-heat oven to 275 °F. Using a wet hand, spread the ball by pressing each along the length of the skewers, two inches apart and making each kabab 5 inches long. If using the oven, make 5-inch croquets and arrange on a greased baking tray and brush with a little melted butter. If shallow frying, flatten the balls into 3/4-inch thick patties.

Cooking : Roast in moderately hot tandoor, brushing once with oil for 6-7 minutes until light golden. Put the baking tray in the pre-heated oven and roast for 9-10 minutes. Heat oil in a heavy bottomed saucepan and shallow fry over medium heat until evenly light golden.

To Serve : Make a bed of mint chutney on each of 4 individual plates. Arrange 4 kababs on top and serve with half a boiled egg, an aubergine.

Ashok Hotel, New Delhi.

Kele Ka Kabab

Aromatic and Spicy Real Banana Kababs

Ingredients

Raw Bananas	8 nos.
Onion	100 gm
Green Chillies	10 gm
Ginger	10 gm
Coriander Leaves	10 gm
Garam Masala	5 gm
Bread Crumbs	100 gm
Salt	To taste
Oil	200 ml
Roasted Bengal Gram without skin	50 gm

Preparation time : 45 minutes

Cooking time : 10 minutes

Yield : 4

Preparation

Boil raw bananas and potatoes. Peel and mash them. Chop ginger, coriander leaves, green chillies and onions. Broil the Bengal gram and powder it.

Cooking

To the mashed banana and potato mixture, add onions, green chillies, ginger, coriander, garam masala, bread crumbs, salt and powdered Bengal gram to make a soft dough. Adjust seasoning. Shape into *Tikkis*. Heat oil in a heavy bottomed pan and shallow fry the *Tikkis* over medium heat until golden brown and crisp on both sides. Press with a spatula and remove.

To Serve

Arrange *Tikkis* on a serving dish and serve with chutney.

Ashok Hotel, New Delhi.

Jimikand Ki Shammi

An exotic kabab flavoured with a unique combination of clove,
nutmeg and mace

Ingredients	
Yam Jimikand	500 gm
Potatoes	450 gm
Black Pepper Powder	3 gm
Red Chilli Powder	3 gm
Cumin Powder	3 gm
Black Cardamom Powder	1 gm
Cinnamon Powder	1 gm
Royal Cumin Powder (Shahi Jeera)	1 gm
Green Cardamom Powder	1 gm
Clove Powder	1 gm
Nutmeg Powder	1 gm
Mace Powder	1 gm
Salt	To taste
Cooking oil to shallow fry Shaami	
The Filling	
Onion	100 gm
Ginger	20 gm
Coriander	20 gm
Green Chillies	2
Lemon Juice	20 ml
The Accompaniments	
Tomatoes	2
Cucumber Slices	8

Preparation time : 35-40 minutes

Cooking Time : 4-5 minutes for each set of 4

Yield : 4

Preparation

Peel the yam, cut into 2 inch pieces, boil, cool and grate. Boil the potatoes, cool peel and mash. Put yam and potatoes in a bowl, add the spices and mix well. Divide into 16 equal portions and make balls.

For Filling

Peel, wash and finely chop onions, scrape, wash and finely chop ginger. Clean, wash and finely chop coriander. Remove stems, stir, deseed, wash and finely chop green chillies. Put these ingredients in a bowl, add lemon juice, mix well and divide into 16 equal portions. Flatten each ball between the palms, place a portion of the filling in the middle, make balls again and flatten into 5/8 - inch thick patties. Halve the tomatoes.

Cooking

Heat oil in a frying pan, shallow fry the patties over medium heat until golden brown and crisp on both sides. Remove and place on absorbent paper.

To Serve

Arrange 4 kababs on each of 4 individual plates and serve with a tomato halve, slices of cucumber.

Ashok Hotel, New Delhi

Tapioca Avial

An Exquisite Delicacy of Tapioca Simmered in Yoghurt Masala

Ingredients

Tapioca	450 gm
Green Chillies	3 nos.
Turmeric Powder	A little
Curry Leaf	A sprig
Ginger	10 gm
Coconut	120 gm
Cumin Seeds	3 gm
Coconut Oil	30 ml
Yoghurt	100 ml

Preparation time : 30 minutes

Cooking time : 20 minutes

Yield : 4

Preparation

Remove the outer skin and inner skin of the tapioca. Cut into long thin pieces. Wash well. Grind grated coconut, cumin seeds and ginger pieces coarsely.

Cooking

Boil the tapioca till tender. Take care to change the water 2-3 times to remove the bitter taste from the tapioca. Heat coconut oil in a thick bottomed pan and add turmeric powder and cooked tapioca. Add the ground masala, yoghurt and curry leaves. Mix well. Add salt. Adjust seasoning.

To Serve

Serve hot with plain rice.

Kovalam Ashok Beach Resort.

Vegetable Tak-A-Tin

A Delectable Exotic Vegetarian Preparation

Ingredients	
Small Brinjal	100 gm
Colocatia	100 gm
Lotus Stem	100 gm
Potato	100 gm
Green Peas	100 gm
Cottage Cheese	100 gm
Tomato Paste	200 gm
Onions	50 gm
Coriander Leaves	10 gm
Green Chillies	2 gm
Salt	to taste
Cooking Oil	75 ml
Red Chilly Powder	2 gm
Turmeric Powder	2 gm
Coriander Powder	3 gm
Garam Masala	2 gm
Chaat Masala	2 gm
Ginger	10 gm

Preparation time : 30 minutes

Cooking Time : 30 minutes

Yield : 4

Preparation

Clean the small brinjal in running water. Peel and cut colocatia in halves.

Clean lotus stem cut diagnally in 1" shape. Cut potatoes into cubes and keep in cold water. Cut cottage cheese in cubes and keep. Chop green coriander, green chillies and chop tomatoes and onions. Finely slice ginger.

Cooking

Fry small brinjal, lotus stem, colocatia and potato. Boil green peas. Sprinkle with salt and chaat masala.

Take a pan. Add oil to it. Add tomato dices and onion to it and cook. Add red chilly powder, dhania powder, turmeric powder, garam masala and make a thick gravy. Add the vegetables into gravy and simmer.

To Serve

Serve in hot plate garnished with green coriander and finely sliced ginger.

Ashok Hotel, New Delhi

Jack Fruit Simmered in a Thick Coconut Flavoured Gravy

Ingredients

Raw Jackfruit without Seed	450 gm
Coconut	1/2 no.
Green Chillies	3 nos.
Turmeric Powder	3 gm
Onion	115 gm
Cumin seeds	3 gm
Garlic	5 gm
Red Chillies Whole	6 nos.
Curry Leaves	A sprig
Madras Onion	3 nos.
Mustard Seeds	3 nos.
Coconut Oil	20 ml
Oil	30 ml

Preparation time : 1 hour 30 minutes

Cooking time : 10 minutes

Yield: 4

Preparation

Using a little oil on the fingers and palm, remove the skin and stem of the jackfruit and cut into small pieces. Chop onion, green chillies and garlic and Madras onion and grate coconut.

Cooking

Boil jackfruit pieces with little turmeric and strain the water. Grind it coarsely. Heat oil and fry chopped ingredients. Add turmeric powder. Add the jackfruit. Add grated coconut and salt. Mix well. Add curry leaves and remove.

Take little coconut oil in a frying pan and heat lightly. Add chopped Madras onion. Stir and add mustard seeds, red chillies whole. When it is brown add to the Thoran. Mix well. Adjust seasoning.

To Serve

Thoran is served with rice.

Kovalam Ashok Beach Resort.

Handi Kofta

A Vegetarian Delight

Ingredients	
For Koftas	
Potatoes	500 gm
Coriander Leaves	20 gm
Ginger	5 gm
Carrot	50 gm
French Beans	50 gm
Green Peas	50 gm
Mushrooms	50 gm
Spinach	75 gm
Salt	To taste
Cornflour	20 gm
Refined Oil	To fry
Cumin Seeds	5 gm
For Gravy	
Onion	150 gm
Tomatoes	150 gm
Turmeric Powder	5 gm
Cumin Seeds	10 gm
Red Chilly Powder	5 gm
Garam Masala	5 gm
Ginger	10 gm
Garlic	5 gm
Refined Oil	50 gm
Yoghurt	50 gm
Water	As required
Salt	To taste

Preparation time : 45 minutes

Cooking time : 45 minutes

Yield : 4

Preparation

Boil potatoes. Peel the skin off, mash it and keep aside. Chop carrot, french beans, mushrooms and spinach. Make ginger-garlic paste.

Cooking

Heat oil in a heavy-bottomed pan and add cumin seeds. Add ginger-garlic paste and chopped vegetables. Cook it well. Make ball shape of mashed potatoes after mixing little cornflour. Stuff the vegetable mixture in the mashed potatoes. Fry in hot oil. Cut the centre and keep it aside. Heat oil, add cumin seeds. When the seeds crackle, add the onions and fry till golden brown. Add ginger-garlic paste and the masalas. Now add the tomatoes and the yoghurt, add salt, water and cook till the gravy is smooth and oil starts leaving the sides.

Add the prepared koftas and simmer for a few minutes till the gravy gets absorbed.

To Serve

Garnish with chopped green coriander and serve hot.

Ashok Hotel, New Delhi.

Dal Makhani

A Creamed Lentil Delicacy

Ingredients	
Urad Dal	120 gm (whole)
Red Kidney Beans	30 gm
Ginger Paste	20 gm
Salt	To taste
Garlic Paste	20 gm
Tomato Puree	120 ml
Red Chilli Powder	5 gm
White Butter	120 gm
Cream	120 ml
Water	1 litres

Preparation time : 15 minutes

Cooking time : 3 hours

Yield : 4

Preparation

Pick and wash in lentils in running water and soak overnight. Drain.

Cooking

Put the drained lentils in a heavy bottomed pot, add salt and water, bring to boil, cover and simmer until the lentils are cooked and two-thirds of the liquid has evaporated. Mash the lentils lightly against the sides with a wooden spoon. Add ginger paste, garlic paste, tomato puree, red chillies and a knob of butter, stir and cook for 45 minutes. Then add cream, stir and cook for 10 minutes. Adjust the seasoning.

To Serve

Remove to a bowl, garnish with the remaining butter and serve with Tandoori Roti.

Ashok Hotel, New Delhi.

Chatpati Sabzi Biryani

Assortment of Vegetables mixed with Rice

Ingredients

Basmati Rice	200 gm
Carrots	50 gm
Green Peas (shelled)	30 gm
Beans	50 gm
Onion Slices	100 gm
Cauliflower	50 gm
Potatoes	30 gm
Ginger	10 gm
Garlic	10 gm
Green Chillies (chopped)	4 nos.
Green Coriander Leaves	15 gm
Tomatoes	150 gm
Coriander Powder	10 gm
Red Chilli Powder	6 gm
Salt	To taste
Turmeric Powder	3 gm
Bay Leaf	2 nos
Cinnamon 1" stick	2 nos
Cardamom Green	4 nos
Cloves	4 nos
Cumin	5 gm
Oil	100 gm
Mint Leaves	15 gm
Lemon	2 nos

Preparation time : 1 hour

Cooking time : 45 minutes

Yield : 4

Preparation : Pick, wash basmati rice and soak in cold water for hour. Remove string from french beans, peel carrots and potatoes and cut the vegetables in dices. Wash, break cauliflower into florets. Scrape ginger, remove skin from garlic, wash and make both pastes seperately. Wash, slit, deseed and chop green chillies, chop coriander and mint leaves, wash and chop tomatoes.

Method : Heat oil in a pan, add the cinnamon, cardamom, cloves, bay leaf. Add the cumin seeds and when they crackle, add onions. Fry well till the onion are golden brown. Now add the ginger, garlic, green chillies, tomatoes, coriander powder, chilli powder, salt, turmeric. Fry well till the masala is well cooked. Use water to prevent masala from sticking on the pot if required. Now add the carrots, beans, peas, cauliflower and potatoes and toss these well in masala, cook till half done. Similarly boil the rice in double the quantity of water. Strain the water immediately, cover the vegetables with the rice. Sprinkle chopped coriander, mint and lemon juice on top. Seal the edges and put in hot oven for 20-25 minutes.

To Serve: Remove the lid and serve hot.

Ashok Hotel, New Delhi.

Naan

A simple, but delicious, unleavened flour bread, garnished with onion seeds and melon seeds

Ingredients

Flour	500 gm
Soda bi-carb	1 gm
Salt	10 gm
Baking Powder	1 tsp
Egg	1 no.
Sugar	10 gm
Yoghurt	2 tbs
Milk	50 ml
Water	200 ml
Oil	25 ml
Flour	To dust
Oil	To grease baking tray
Onion Seeds	1 tsp
Melon Seeds	5 gm
Butter	30 gm

Preparation time : 2 hours 30 minutes

Cooking time : 20 minutes

Yield : 6

Preparation

Sieve the flour with salt, soda bi-carb and baking powder into a flat dish. Break the egg in a bowl, add sugar, yoghurt and milk. Whisk. Make a bay in the sieved flour, pour water in it and start mixing gradually. When fully mixed, knead to make a dough. Add the egg mixture and incorporate gradually. When fully mixed, knead to make a soft dough, cover with a moist cloth and keep aside for 10 minutes. Then add oil, knead and punch the dough, cover with a moist cloth and keep aside for 2 hours to allow the dough to rise.

Divide into 6 equal portions, make balls and place on a lightly floured surface. Sprinkle onion and melon seeds, flatten the balls slightly, cover and keep aside for 5 minutes. Flatten each ball between the palms to make a round disc and then stretch on one side in the shape of an elongated oval.

Cooking

Place the Naan on a cushioned pad, stick inside a moderately hot tandoor and bake for 3 minutes.

To Serve

Apply butter on Naan as soon as it is removed from the tandoor, and serve immediately.

Ashok Hotel, New Delhi.

Sheermal

Sheermal is a rich bread, its quality judged by the amount of fat incorporated in the dough.

Ingredients

Flour	500 gm
Salt	To taste
Warm Milk	500 ml
Sugar	10 gm
Rose Water	2 drops
Clarified Butter	1 cup
Flour	To dust
Saffron	1 gm

Preparation time : 1 hour 30 minutes

Cooking time : 8-10 minutes

Yield : 12

Preparation

Sieve the flour with salt into a flat dish. Dissolve the sugar in 400 ml warm milk, reserve the rest to dissolve saffron.

Make a bay in the sieved flour, pour the milk in it and start mixing gradually. When fully mixed, knead to make a dough, cover with a moist cloth and keep aside for 10 minutes. Add the clarified butter and incorporate gradually. When fully mixed, knead to make a soft dough, cover and keep aside for 10 minutes. Divide into 12 equal portions, make balls, dust with flour, cover and keep aside for 10 minutes. Place the balls on a lightly floured surface and flatten each with a rolling pin into round discs (approx 7" diameter). Prick the entire surface with a fork. Dissolve the saffron in the warm reserved milk.

Cooking

Pre-heat the oven to 350 ° F. Grease a baking tray with clarified butter, arrange the discs on it and bake in the pre-heated oven for 4 minutes. Remove, brush immediately with saffron, return to the oven and bake for 3-4 minutes.

To Serve

Brush Sheermal with clarified butter as soon as it is removed from the oven and serve immediately.

Ashok Hotel, New Delhi.

Khameeri Roti

Khameeri means leavened, which makes this a rare whole-wheat bread. A combination of yoghurt, whole-wheat flour and sugar makes the flour rise and provides it a distinct flavour.

Ingredients

Whole-wheat Flour	500 gm
Salt	A pinch
Water	200 ml
Yoghurt	250 ml
Sugar	10 gm
Flour	To dust

Preparation time : 1 hour 20 minutes

Cooking time : 3-4 minutes

Yield : 8

Preparation

Sieve the whole-wheat flour with salt into a flat dish. Make a bay in the sieved whole-wheat flour, pour water and yoghurt in it and start mixing gradually. When fully mixed, knead to make a hard dough, cover with a moist cloth and keep aside for 15 minutes. Knead until the dough is not sticky. Cover and keep in a warm place for 30 minutes to allow the dough to rise. Divide into 8 portions, make balls, dust with flour, cover and keep aside for 5 minutes.

Cooking

Flatten each ball between the palms to make a round disc (approx 9-inch diameter), place the Roti on a cushioned pad, stick inside a moderately hot tandoor and bake for 3-4 minutes.

To Serve

Serve as soon as it is removed from the tandoor.

Ashok Hotel, New Delhi.

Tandoori Roti

The common unleavened whole-wheat flour bread, popular with North Indians

Ingredients	
Whole-wheat Flour	550 gm
Salt	10 gm
Water	350 ml

Preparation time : 40 minutes

Cooking time : In Tandoor: 2 minutes

Yield : 8

Preparation

Sieve the whole-wheat flour with salt into a flat dish. Make a bay in the sieved flour, pour water in it and start mixing gradually. When fully mixed, knead to make a soft dough, cover with a moist cloth and keep aside for 30 minutes. Divide into 8 equal portions, make balls.

Cooking

Flatten each ball between the palms to make a round disc (approx 6-inch diameter), place the Roti on a cushioned pad, stick inside a moderately hot tandoor or oven and bake for 2 minutes.

To Serve

Serve as soon as it is removed from the tandoor or oven.

Ashok Hotel, New Delhi.

South Indian Paratha

A Flaky Paratha

Ingredients	
Flour	500 gm
Soda bi-carb	A pinch
Milk	150 ml
Sugar	10 g
Salt	To taste
Groundnut oil	60 ml
Butter	100 gm
Ghee	To shallow fry

Preparation time : 50 minutes

Cooking time : 30 minutes

Yield : 4

Preparation

Sieve the flour with soda bi-carb into a flat dish. Add milk, sugar, salt and oil. Whisk. Make a bay in the sieved flour, pour the milk mixture in it and start mixing gradually. When fully mixed, knead to make a soft dough. Keep aside for 30 minutes.

Divide the dough into 6 equal portions and make balls. Flatten each with hand. Grease the rolling surface with oil. Place the flattened dough and stretch evenly on all sides until it is very thin (approx. 15 inch diameter). Apply melted butter over the entire surface , hold from two ends and gather ensuring there are many folds. Place the dough on the table. Flatten each ball into round shape of 6" diameter. Dust with flour while rolling.

Cooking

Place Paratha on a heated hot plate and half-bake turning over once. Pour melted fat all round and shallow fry both sides over low heat until golden brown.

To Serve

Remove and serve immediately.

Kovalam Ashok Beach Resort.

Phirni

A popular dessert, set in SHIKORAS — earthenware bowls and flavoured with cardamom and saffron

Ingredients

Milk	1 litre
Basmati Rice	50 gm
Sugar	250 gm
Saffron	1 gm
Green Cardamom Powder	1 tsp
Rosewater Concentrate	2 drops
Pistachio	2 tsp
Almonds	10 gm

Preparation time: 40 minutes

Cooking time: 15 minutes

Yield : 4

Preparation

Pick, wash the rice in running water and soak for 30 minutes. Drain, put in a blender, add water and make a fine paste.

Blanch pistachio and almonds; cool, remove the skin and cut into half.

Rinse the *shikoras* in running water and put them in a deep pan full of water. Remove and pat dry.

Cooking

Boil the milk in a deep pan, add the rice paste and sugar whilst stirring with a whisk. Reduce to low heat and cook, stirring constantly (to ensure no lumps are formed), until the mixture becomes thick and is reduced to a custard consistency. Add saffron, cardamom and rosewater concentrate, stir and remove.

Assembling

Pour equal quantities of Phirni in the *Shikoras*, garnish with pistachio and almonds and refrigerate until set.

To Serve

Remove *shikoras* from refrigerator and serve cold.

Ashok Hotel, New Delhi.

Rasmalai

Sweet and Soft Cottage Cheese Balls in Rabarhi — A Traditional Bengali Sweet Meal

Ingredients

Ingredients	
Cow's milk	1.5 litre
Soured Casein	30 ml
Flour	15 gm
Baking Powder	1 gm
Sugar	750 gm
Rabarhi (unsweetened)	500 gm
Water	1380 ml
Pistachio	5 gm

Preparation time : 30 minutes plus time taken for Rabarhi

Cooking time : 30 minutes

Yield : 4

Preparation : Boil milk, reduce heat, add soured casein and pour the curdled milk through a muslin cloth to make *Chhenna*. Knead gently to mash any granules. Sieve 10 gm of flour and baking powder together, mix with *Chhenna* and knead to make a dough. Divide into 12 equal portions, make balls and gently squeeze between the palms and flatten to make 'patties' (approx. 1 " diameter), ensuring that the surface is smooth. Dissolve the remaining flour in 30 ml of water.

The Rabarhi : Add 150 gm. of sugar while it is still warm and stir until dissolved. Cool and refrigerate in the serving bowl. Blanch the pistachio, cool and remove the skin and cut into slivers.

Cooking : Dissolve the remaining sugar in water (approx. 400 ml) and bring to a boil, add the dissolved flour and when the syrup rises, add the 'patties' and poach over high heat for 10 minutes. This is a tricky operation because under no circumstances should the syrup be allowed to settle down. To maintain the consistency, add water (approx. 180 ml) in a steady trickle. To ascertain whether the Rasmalai is cooked, remove one in a spoon and look closely for perforations, akin to those in a sponge, which will appear on the surface for only a second.

Fill water (approx. 800 ml) in a separate pan, transfer Rasmalai, alongwith the syrup. Cool, dip in Rabarhi and refrigerate.

To Serve : Remove from the refrigerator, garnish with pistachio and serve cold.

Ashok Hotel, New Delhi.

Shahi Tukrha

A Classic Dessert

Ingredients

Rabarhi (unsweetened)	150 gm
Green Cardamom Powder	4 gm
Sliced Milk Bread	4 nos
Groundnut Oil	To deep fry
Milk	250 ml
Water	150 ml
Sugar	200 gm
Rose water	A few drops
Almonds	10 gm
Pistachio	5 gm
Saffron	1 gm

Preparation time : 1 hour fifteen minutes plus time taken for Rabarhi.

Yield : 4

Preparation

The Rabarhi : Add sugar in warm milk and stir until dissolved.

The syrup : Boil the sugar remaining with water (400 ml approx.) to make a syrup of one-string consistency. Add cardamom powder.

The Bread : Slice off the crust. Heat oil in a frying pan and deep fry over low heat until golden brown and crisp. Boil the milk in a large, flat, thick bottomed pan. Immerse the fried bread in the remaining milk, the slices at least an inch apart. Return the pan to heat and simmer until the milk is absorbed, turning once in between with a spatula without breaking the bread. Remove from heat and pour on the warm syrup.

Blanch almonds and pistachio, cool, remove the skin and cut into slivers.

Dissolve the saffron in the reserved milk while it is still warm.

Arrange the soaked Tukrha on a platter, spread Rabarhi on top, garnish with nuts and sprinkle saffron and rose water.

To Serve

Serve cold, garnish with almonds and pistachio.

Ashok Hotel, New Delhi

Rabarhi

Sweetened & Thickened Milk Dessert

Ingredients	
Milk	2 litres
Sugar	200 gm
Rosewater	5 drops

Preparation time : 5 minutes

Cooking time : 2 hours

Yield : 1/2 kg

Preparation
Blanch the pistachio, cool, remove the skin and cut into slivers.

Cooking
Put milk in a heavy bottomed pan, bring to a boil, reduce to low heat and stir constantly for 20 minutes. Then stir after every 5 minutes until milk is reduced to 900ml/3 ∫ cups and acquires granular consistency. Remove, add sugar and stir until dissolved. Then add rosewater and stir. Cool, remove to a silver bowl, garnish with pistachio and refrigerate.

To Serve
Serve chilled.

Ashok Hotel, New Delhi

Kulfi *(Kesar-Pista)*

A rich ice-cream flavoured in saffron and pistachio

Ingredients

Rabarhi	500 gm
Sugar	200 gm
Pistachio	15 gm
Saffron	1 gm
Milk	10 ml
Green Cardamom Powder	2 gm
Falooda for Garnishing	
Rose Syrup for Topping	

Preparation time : 10 minutes (plus time taken for Rabarhi and Falooda)

Freezing time : 6 hours

Yield : 4

Preparation

Blanch the pistachios, cool, remove the skin and cut into slivers. Dissolve saffron in warm milk.

To the rabarhi add sugar, pistachio, saffron and cardamom while it is still warm and stir until sugar is dissolved. Cool.

Assembling

Put rabarhi in kulfi moulds or in ice-creams mould and freeze.

To Serve

Demould, slice into half vertically, garnish with Falooda, top with rose syrup and serve.

Ashok Hotel, New Delhi.

Falooda

A Noodle-like Garnish made with Cornflour and served with Kulfi

Ingredients

Ingredients	
Cornflour	200 gm
Water	750 ml

Preparation time: 40 minutes

Yield : approx 800 gms

Preparation

Put cornflour in a heavy bottomed pan, add water and stir until dissolved. Then cook over medium heat, stirring constantly, until reduced to a gelatinous consistency. Force the cooked cornflour immediately through a Falooda machine/Noodle press using the 1/16-inch mesh and collect the Falooda in a pan full of chilled water.

Ashok Hotel, New Delhi.